05 1793

CHILDRENS AREA

DATE DUE

JUN 1 1 2005	
JUN 2 9 2005	
JUL 2 0 2005	
SEP 2 2 2005	
OCT 2 6 2005	
NOV 0 8 2005	
DEC 1 6 2005	
APR 2 7 2006	
MAY 1 0 2007	
GAYLORD	PRINTED IN U.S.A.

Let's Read About Insects
BUTTERFLIES

by Susan Ashley

Reading consultant: Susan Nations, M.Ed., author/literacy coach/consultant

WEEKLY **WR** READER®
EARLY LEARNING LIBRARY

Please visit our web site at: **www.earlyliteracy.cc**
For a free color catalog describing Weekly Reader® Early Learning Library's
list of high-quality books, call 1-877-445-5824 (USA) or 1-800-387-3178 (Canada).
Weekly Reader® Early Learning Library's fax: (414) 336-0164.

Library of Congress Cataloging-in-Publication Data

Ashley, Susan.
    Butterflies / by Susan Ashley.
      p. cm. — (Let's read about insects)
    Summary: An introduction to the physical characteristics and behavior of butterflies.
    Includes bibliographical references and index.
    ISBN 0-8368-4052-6 (lib. bdg.)
    ISBN 0-8368-4059-3 (softcover)
    1. Butterflies—Juvenile literature. (1. Butterflies.) I. Title.
QL544.2.A84   2004
595.78—dc22   2003062190

This edition first published in 2004 by
Weekly Reader® Early Learning Library
330 West Olive Street, Suite 100
Milwaukee, WI 53212 USA

Copyright © 2004 by Weekly Reader® Early Learning Library

Editor: JoAnn Early Macken
Picture research: Diane Laska-Swanke
Art direction and page layout: Tammy Gruenewald

Picture credits: Cover, pp. 7, 9, 13, 15 © Brian Kenney; title, pp. 5, 17 © Diane Laska-Swanke;
p. 11 © William Weber/Visuals Unlimited; p. 19 © Fritz Polking/Visuals Unlimited; p. 21
© Robert & Linda Mitchell

Printed in the United States of America

1 2 3 4 5 6 7 8 9 08 07 06 05 04

Note to Educators and Parents

Reading is such an exciting adventure for young children! They are beginning to integrate their oral language skills with written language. To encourage children along the path to early literacy, books must be colorful, engaging, and interesting; they should invite the young reader to explore both the print and the pictures.

Let's Read About Insects is a new series designed to help children read about insect characteristics, life cycles, and communities. In each book, young readers will learn interesting facts about the featured insects and how they live.

Each book is specially designed to support the young reader in the reading process. The familiar topics are appealing to young children and invite them to read — and reread — again and again. The full-color photographs and enhanced text further support the student during the reading process.

In addition to serving as wonderful picture books in schools, libraries, homes, and other places where children learn to love reading, these books are specifically intended to be read within an instructional guided reading group. This small group setting allows beginning readers to work with a fluent adult model as they make meaning from the text. After children develop fluency with the text and content, the book can be read independently. Children and adults alike will find these books supportive, engaging, and fun!

— Susan Nations, M.Ed., author, literacy coach,
and consultant in literacy development

All insects change as they grow. No insect changes as much as a butterfly.

Butterflies lay their eggs on leaves. They choose leaves that are good to eat. The eggs hatch. The larvae crawl out. They are known as **caterpillars**.

The caterpillars eat the leaves. They shed their old skin as they grow. Then they grow new skin.

A caterpillar eats and grows for a few weeks. Then it attaches itself to a twig or a leaf. It hangs upside down. It sheds its skin one last time.

A new form appears.
The new form is called
a **pupa**, or **chrysalis**.
This one looks like a
light green shell. The
shell breaks open.
A butterfly comes out!

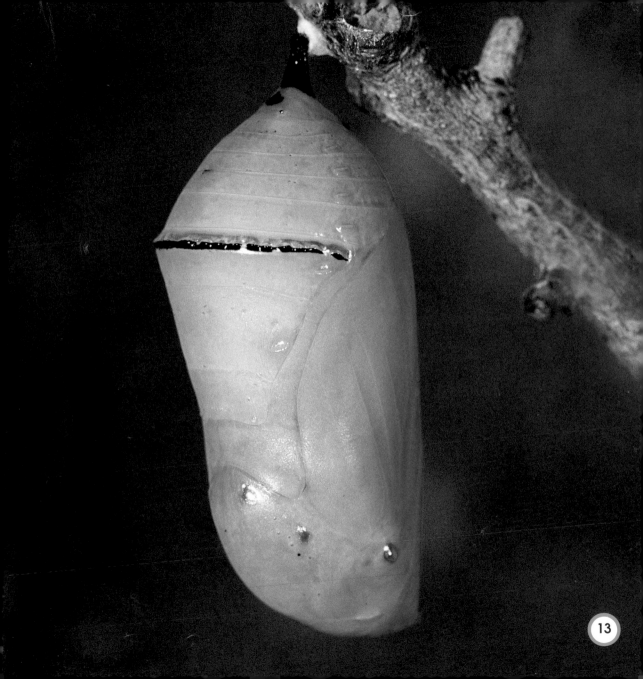

Tiny scales cover a butterfly's wings. The scales give wings their colors. The colors form patterns on the wings.

A butterfly can fly only when its body is warm. Butterflies are usually seen on warm, sunny days. They are not often seen on cold, cloudy days.

Winter is hard on butterflies. Some hibernate in safe places. Others migrate. They fly to find warm weather. They may fly thousands of miles.

In spring, warm weather returns. Butterflies emerge from their chrysalises. They mate and lay eggs. The butterfly life cycle begins again.

Glossary

chrysalis — a butterfly in its third stage of growth

hibernate — to spend the winter resting, without eating

larvae — insects in their second stage of growth

migrate — to travel from one region or climate to another on a regular schedule

scales — small, flat plates that cover part of an animal's body

For More Information

Books

Coleman, Graham. *Butterflies.* Milwaukee: Gareth Stevens, 1997.

Frost, Helen. *Caterpillars.* Mankato: Capstone Press, 2000.

Schwartz, David M. *Monarch Butterfly.* Milwaukee: Gareth Stevens, 1999.

Wallace, Karen. *Born to be a Butterfly.* New York: DK Publishing, 2000.

Web Sites

Butterflies at the Field Museum
www.fmnh.org/butterfly/default.htm
Facts and photographs from the Field Museum

Index

About the Author

Susan Ashley has written over eighteen books for children, including two picture books about dogs, *Puppy Love* and *When I'm Happy, I Smile*. She enjoys animals and writing about them. Susan lives in Wisconsin with her husband and two frisky felines.